PHP: ACQUIRE A SOLID UNDERSTANDING OF PHP IN ONE DAY. BEGINNER'S GUIDE TO PHP USING PROJECT.

2

Contents

3

4

Introduction to PHP

Describe PHP.

- The term "PHP: Hypertext Preprocessor" is an abbreviation.

- A popular open source programming language is PHP.
- On the server, PHP programs are run.
- You may use and download PHP for free.
- PHP is a fantastic and well-liked language!

- It is strong enough to serve as the foundation of WordPress, the largest blogging platform on the internet!
- It has enough depth to power big social networks!

- It is also simple enough to serve as the first server's language for a novice.

How do PHP files work?

Text, HTML, CSS, JavaScript, & PHP code may all be found in PHP files.

PHP scripts contain the extension ".php," and when performed on a server, deliver plain HTML to the browser.

Which build system should (mostly) PHP applications use?

After reading, I concluded that Ping was the best build system for PHP programmers. However, my "friends," who may have been overly (?) influenced by JavaScript, tell me that Gulp is the best option.

I'll use it mostly to compile tools like phpunit, phpdoc, phpcs, phpmd, jcsc, and jshint under one virtual roof. I won't utilize it right now to publish files to a distant server. It is only used for testing, statist code checking, style sheet compilation and compression, Travis/Scrutinizer testing, and...

I have no problem utilizing Gulp, Ping, or any other well-known and established build system. But picking a suitable approach would be wonderful.

What is your opinion, and/or what do you personally recommend?

How can I locate the SQL source code?

There is no need to use another view in SQL Server because the source code for stored processes and functions is also located in the ROUTINE_DEFINITION field of the INFORMATION_SCHEMA

ROUTINES. This RDBMS includes the complete statement, including CREATE PROCEDURE and its parameters.

What are the drawbacks of DBMS packages?

Advantages of the Package - Using Oracle PL/SQL packages may result in the Oracle database server using more memory since the whole package is loaded into memory whenever any item in the package is accessed.

Why do we utilize SQL packages?

Packages provide a practical method of classifying the operations and processes that serve the same function. One permission that is given to the whole package determines whether someone is allowed to utilize the package's functions and processes. A package's contents may have certain things designated as public.

The best option is a bundle or a technique.

Data transmission will be handled by your method. Such procedures carry out actions that are connected to one another, and a package is a database item that may include numerous of them. By not disclosing your method in the package definition, you may make it private to the package.

What does SQL source code mean?

Data analyst source code example SQL

The building of data tables or queries of them are both examples of source code in SQL. However, since searching a database lacks innovation, it is less effective than generating. Data may be accessed by anybody, but it cannot be produced by everyone.

How many a SQL database be queried for data?

SELECT clauses

A database table's entries are retrieved using a SQL SELECT statement in accordance with clauses (such FROM and WHERE) that define criteria. As for the syntax: the following query: SELECT column1, column2 FROM table1, table2 On column2='value';

How can I get the MySQL source code?

View the Source

Download the MySQL Servers documentation from https://dev.mysql.com/downloads /mysql in order to build MySQL Router. Alternative: git clone GitHub's mysql-server repository.

How can I create a SQL script?

5.5. 1 Using the Script Editor to Create a SQL Script

Click SQL Workshop, followed by SQL Scripts, on the Workspace homepage. The page for SQL Scripts appears.

Select "Create" from the menu.

Enter a name for the script in the Script Name field.

Put in the SQL and PL/SQL blocks that you wish to use in your script.

Press Create.

Run SQL Server unit tests via the Test Explorer in Visual Studio 2012

After choosing Windows from the Test menu, click Test Explorer.

Test Explorer's window appears.

By clicking on them in the Test Explorer, you may choose the test(s) you want to perform. Using the CTRL or SHIFT keys, you may design tests that have irregular or consistent parts.

By clicking on one of the tests that is highlighted, you may choose Run Selected Tests from the context menu.

Use the SQL Server Unit Test Designer in Visual Studio 2010 to execute SQL Server unit tests.

On the Test Tools toolbar, there are buttons to start a task with or without the debugger.

At this stage, every test in the current test run is performed. As soon as you start the test run, the Test Results window, which displays its status, appears. This display includes both tests that are still running and those that have already concluded.

How can I correct SQL mistakes?

Check the wording on the line in your SQL query that is failing. Review the line where your SQL query is failing for any missing brackets or commas. Eliminate commented lines, which are those that start with -- or /*. Look through your SQL dialect for typical syntax mistakes.

What exactly is data cleansing?

The process of rectifying faulty, insufficient, duplicate, or other incorrect data during information collecting is known as data cleansing, often referred to as data cleaning, data scrubbing, or data rectification. It involves identifying data errors and fixing them by altering, updating, or removing data. Data cleaning improves data quality and helps provide more accurate, reliable, and consistent information for internal decision-making inside a company.

Data cleaning, which is an essential stage in the overall data management process, is part of the preparation work that gets data sets ready for use for analytical (BI) and the information science applications. The people who carry it out are often quality regarding data analysts, engineers, along with additional data management specialists. Data scientists, BI economists, and customers may potentially clean data or take part in the process for their own applications.

Data scrubbing vs data cleaning versus data cleansing

Data scrubbing, data cleaning, and data cleansing are often used synonymously. They are often regarded as being the same item. Data scrubbing, however, is often seen as a component of data cleaning that focuses especially on eliminating redundant, flawed, unnecessary, or outdated data from data sets.

A distinct definition of data cleansing applies when talking about data storage. In that sense, it refers to an automated procedure that examines storage devices like disk drives to ensure that the data they contain can be read and to spot any defective sectors or blocks.

How is the SQLite extension loaded?

An Extension's Load

The name of the file hosting the shared library or DLL and an entry suggest initialize the extension must be provided to SQLite in order to load it. This data is provided via the sqlite3_load_extension() API in C. For further details, see the documentation for that procedure.

How can I make SQL extensions active?

If the required files are not included in the normal distribution, you must download and install them before you can activate and use an extension. To accomplish this, use a SQL client like psql and run the command CREATE EXTENSION name>;. Use the dx command in psql to manage the extensions that are already installed.

How are PECL extensions installed?

Installing the PECL extensions required by Debian. install make, install php5-dev, and install php-pear through apt-get.

Syntax for PECL. Installing the PECL Extension Syntax install extname-ver using pecl.

Activate PHP5's PECL Extension using the PECL Extension Install Example.
Turn on the Extension.
Cleaning up.
Verify.

PHP 5.X installation of the SQLSRV Extension

PHP 5.X is no longer supported by this extension.

Inspection of the Installation

With the following command, you can confirm the SQLSRV extension is set up:

sqlsrv:php7.X-sp -i | grep
If SQLSRV is successfully installed, the following will appear:

/etc/php7.1-sp/conf.d/pdo_sqlsrv.ini,
/etc/php7.1-sp/conf.d/sqlsrv.ini,
Registered PHP Streams => http, ftp, zip, phar, compress.zlib, compress.bzip2, php, file, glob, sqlsrv
Drivers for PDO pgsql, sqlite, dblib, mysql, odbc, and sqlsrv
pdo_sqlsrv
pdo_sqlsrv support => enabled
pdo_sqlsrv.client_buffer_max_kb_siz e => 10240 => 10240
pdo_sqlsrv.log_severity => 0 => 0
sqlsrv sqlsrv support => enabled
sqlsrv.ClientBufferMaxKBSize => 10240 => 10240 sqlsrv How to Remove the SQLSRV Extension

Run the following commands as root to remove this extension:

Run "sudo rm /etc/phpX."sudo rm /etc/phpX Y-sp/conf.d/sqlsrv.ini.sudo peclX Y-sp/conf.d/pdo_sqlsrv.ini.sudo y-sp sqlsrv uninstall peclX.Y-sp remove pdo_sqlsrv

Then, restart PHP-FPM using the following command:

Service sudo start phpX.Y-fpm-sp.

Extensions that improve the PHP source tree

A PHP extension and a third-party extension are the same in every manner. As a result, developing an external extra is as easy as copying the file into the PHP source tree and using the default build instructions.

To demonstrate this, we'll utilize APCu as an example.

The PHP source tree's ext/EXTNAME directory must initially include the extension's source code. If the extension can be accessed by git, all that is needed is to clone the archive from inside ext/.

Go to https://github.com/krakjoe/apcu.git and run git clone "/php-src/ext" You may also download and unzip a source tarball as an alternative:

wget tar xzf apcu-4.0.2.tgz in /tmp mkdir /php-src/ext/apcu, cp -r apcu-4.0.2, http://pecl.php.net/get/apcu-4.0.2.tgz, and apcu-4.0.2/ The extension will include the config.m4 file, which specifies extension-specific build instructions for use by autoconf. To include them in the./configure script, you have to run./buildconf one a little longer. It is suggested to first delete the configuration file to confirm if it was generated:

In php-src, remove configure and./buildconf.
Using the./config.nice script, you may now add APCu to the current configuration, or you can start again with a new configure line:

either /php-src/./config.nice -- enable-apcu # or /php-src/./configure --enable-apcu #
Finally, launch make -jN to finish the build. Since we didn't use --enable-apcu=shared, the extension is statically tied into the PHP binary

and can thus be used without further action. Naturally, make install may also be used to install the created binaries.

Making and Setting Up a PHP Extension

Without making any modifications, this extension skeleton may be built. The PHP construct we made in the first stage includes the first "phpize" command. The PATH should still include it.

PHPize,./configure, make, and install all cost money.

These instructions should create the "test.so" shared extension and transfer it to the proper directory inside our PHP system. We must add a line to our customized php.ini in order to load it.

Use vi to open /php-bin/DEBUG/etc/php.ini.
the next line, please:

extension=test.So make sure the expansion is loaded and functional. The list of available extensions is shown by the "php -m" command:

$ grep test | php -m test
We could alternatively execute the procedures listed in our "test" extension:

PHP -r 'test_test1();'
The loading and functioning of the extension test!
Echo test_test2("worldn"); using PHP:
Dear World

Now it makes sense to begin utilizing a version control system to keep track of our source code modifications. (I choose GIT.)

git init $
$ git add tests test.c php_test.h config.m4 config.w32
$ git commit The "Initial Extension Skeleton"

How can I locate the PHP extensions directory?

The output of the phpinfo function may be used to locate the location of the ini file (using the method of searching for php. ini in the results of phpinfo function). The variable zend_extension, which is often found at the end of the php. ini file, may be used to place xdebug in a

location other than the extension
directory.

What PHP modules are present?

Checking your server's PHP Information Page, which lists all installed modules and offers a complete overview of your server's PHP settings, is the simplest approach to find out what PHP extensions are installed on your server. This indicates that the "mastering" PHP module was compiled into your server.

PHP's Basic Structure

The PHP script is run by the server, which then sends the browser's HTML output. Tags for HTML and PHP are often present. Hypertext Preprocessor (PHP), a well-liked general-purpose open-source programming language, may be integrated into an HTML document. PHP files are saved with the.php suffix. PHP scripts, ordinary HTML, and other code may be written in PHP tags.

PHP is a comfortable language to use, whether you're an expert or a newbie. In the first level of this PHP tutorial series, we begin using PHP. Even more seasoned developers who need retraining are excellent to start from scratch. You'll often find that complex problems are frequently just very simple errors. The importance of the basics is due to this. They serve as the cornerstone for expanding your overall programming knowledge. So let's get our hands dirty with PHP today as we examine what it is and the background of this somewhat divisive language.

Examples:-

Body, HTML, and H1 tags are all in the!DOCTYPE html tag.ScmGalaxy</h1>

'Hello ScmGalaxy' is echoed by PHP throughout the code.

</body> </html>

Data Types in PHP

Simple text and numeric data types, as well as more complex data types like arrays and objects, may all have values in PHP variables.

PHP supports a total of eight fundamental data types: integer, float (floating point number), text, boolean, array, protest, resource, and NULL. These data types are used to create variables. Let's now go a little more into each of them.

Python's integers

Integers are whole numbers containing a decimal point, such as -2, -1, 0, 1, 2, etc. Integers may be expressed in three different ways: octal (base 8 - prefixed with 0), hexadecimal (base 16 - prefixed with 0x), and decimal (base 10 - preceded with a sign (- or +) before them).

Run the code shown below:PHP code: $a = 123; // Decimal number var_dump ($a); echo "br>";

echos "br>"; $b = -123; // var_dump ($b) outputs a negative value;

Hexadecimal value $c = 0x1A;
var_dump($c); echo "br>";

octal value $d = 0123 in
var_dump($d);

PHP Strings

Strings are collections of characters, each of which is equivalent to a single byte.

A string may have a maximum size of 2GB (2147483647 bytes) and include letters, integers, and special characters. The easiest approach to express a string is to surround it in single quotations (for example, "Hello world!"). Double quotes are also acceptable.

Run this code as an example

"Hello world! "; echo $a; echo "br>";
php;

"Hello world!" is written in the variable $b.

Stay here, I'll come back. $c = $c; echo $c;?>

PHP Boolean

There are just two possible outcomes for a boolean: 1 (true) or 0 (false).

Execute this code as an example
PHP // Set the variable $show_error to the value TRUE by using var_dump($show_error).

CSS Arrays

An array is a kind of variable that may hold several values

simultaneously. It may be advantageous to unite a group of related things, such as a list of country or city names.

An indexed collection of data objects is the formal definition of an array. All of an array's indexes, also known as its keys, are unique and lead to the same thing.

Run this code as an example.

```php
<?php
$colors contains an array of Red, Green, and Blue colors; var_dump($colors); echo "br>";

"Red" => "#ff0000," "Green" => "#00ff00," and "Blue" => "#0000ff");
var_dump($color_codes);?>
```

How is memory managed by PHP?

The PHP Resource Manager API closely resembles the traditional libc malloc API, however it utilizes a separate heap and is tailored to the needs of PHP. Typically, any RAM allotted for processing requests should be immediately released thereafter.

Can PHP handle its memory?

The MySQL Native Driver calls PHP memory management methods via a small wrapper. The wrapper facilitates debugging among other things. Between driven and unbuffered result sets, different MySQL Server and client APIs make distinctions.\
How does PHP internally manage memory?

PHP uses two allocators: the persistent allocator, which keeps allocations across requests, and the per-request allocator, which releases all memory at the conclusion of a request. The persistent allocator and the standard system allocator function similarly.

What does a PHP reference mean?

In PHP, references allow you to access the exact same variable content using several names. They differ from C pointers in that you cannot use them for pointer arithmetic, they do not represent real memory locations, and so forth. For further information, go to What References Are Not. They are really symbol table aliases.

How does PHP build references?

The same content might have several names in PHP because variable names and variable contents are distinct concepts. By adding the & symbol before the original variable, a link to that variable is established. As a result, if b=&&, bisareferewncevariableofa.

What is a casting operation of type?

The compiler automatically changes one data type in a program to another via a process known as type casting. Type casting is another term for type conversion. For instance, a programmer may type cast a long variable into an int if they wish to save the value of the long variable in a basic integer in their program.

What do PHP casting operators do?

Cast to integer using (int), (integer).
Cast to boolean from (bool), (boolean).
Cast to float using (float), (double), and (real).
Cast to string using (string).
Cast (array) to array.
cast to object (object).
cast to NULL (unset) in PHP 5.

How does PHP's Zend engine operate?

PHP utilizes Zend Engine internally as a compiler works. and runtime engine. Zend epodes are created by compiling PHP scripts into memory. Following the execution of these opcodes, the client receives the HTML that was produced.

How does the Zend engine work?
The Zend PHP Engine is a well-liked option for web developers since it is designed to optimize PHP code and enhance performance. It is open source, free to use, reliable, needs little coding, and just the server fees need to be covered.

Is printf compatible with PHP?
PHP's printf() function

A prepared string was printed using the printf() function. It gives back the output string's length.

In PHP, how do you type printf?
Example of the PHP printf() FunctionPurchase a PHP server.

Make a formatted string available: $number equals 9;...

Using the format value%f, enter the following: $number = 123; printf("%f",$number);...

Placeholder usage: $number equals 123;...

An example of every conceivable format value: $num1 = 123456789;

...

An example of a string specifier: ; $str1 = "Hello"

How does PHP print the function?

One or more strings are printed using the print() method. Note: Since the print() function isn't technically a function, parentheses are not necessary when using it. Note that print() is a little slower than echo().

Benefits of PHP

1. The fact that PHP is open-source and free is its greatest benefit. It may easily be utilized with events or online apps and can be downloaded from anywhere.
2. Platforms don't matter. Applications created with PHP may operate on any OS, including UNIX, Linux, Windows, etc.
3. Applications made using PHP that are linked to a database could load quickly. It is popular because it loads more quickly than other programming languages over sluggish internet connections.
4. It has a lower learning curve and is easier to operate, making it more user-friendly.

Working with PHP shouldn't be difficult for someone who is used to C programming.

5. With the help of keeping support for multiple versions, it is more trustworthy for one or two years.

6. It eliminates the need to develop intricate, protracted code for web application events and makes it simpler to reuse similar code.

7. It simplifies fundamental code management.

8. Strong library support enables the usage of a variety of function modules for information representation.

9. PHP's integrated SQL modules make it simple to link files for developing web apps and content-based

websites, which saves time and effort.

10. The popularity of PHP has led to the emergence of several developer organizations, some of whom may be candidates for employment.

11. PHP is flexible enough to work well with a broad variety of different programming languages, enabling the software to use the most cutting-edge technology for each individual function.

Drawbacks of PHP

We just noted that this language has certain drawbacks, so let's examine them and find out what the typical issues developers encounter with PHP are.

1. Not as adaptable
2. You're ready to go if you just want to utilize this scripting language to create WebPages and web apps. If that's the case, we'd even advise hiring PHP developers from us. However, if your project is bigger and you'll require technologies like big data, artificial intelligence, machine learning, etc. to bring everything to life, you may want to think about using a different programming language.

3. insufficient debugging tools
4. The fact that PHP provides few debugging tools is a widespread gripe among developers. It handles failures badly, particularly when compared to other scripting languages; this is mostly due to the low performance of the debugging tools required to monitor and look for such issues.

5. Unable to change essential behavior
6. If your main objective while working on a job is to make it as creative as possible, PHP is not the right tool for you. This is due to the fact that PHP as a scripting language for web applications does not permit

any alterations or changes to the frameworks governing their fundamental functionality. This implies that you will face certain limitations while attempting to get novel results.

7. Security might be better.
8. PHP has a freely available ASCII text file since the source code is open source. In essence, this implies that whatever code you develop will be freely accessible to the world, along with any defects it may have. Additionally, this implies that they may use such flaws against you. Security is thus not the greatest.

9. Languages that are simpler to use exist.

10.   PHP is a very simple programming language to use. If you are already a developer, you will quickly become proficient. This language, nevertheless, is written like code. Python, on the other hand, is written similarly to English, so even a newbie can understand it. Consequently, even if PHP is simple to comprehend, other languages are simpler.

www.ingramcontent.com/pod-product-compliance
Lightning Source LLC
Chambersburg PA
CBHW071006260726
48661CB00007B/2825